East Dunbartonshire Libraries

3 8060 05898 1291

KU-236-448

Instant Expert

SELF-

Gary Freeman &
Jonathan Bentman

DEFENCE

A & C BLACK

Published by:
A & C Black Publishers Limited
36 Soho Square
London W1D 3QY

www.acblack.com

First published 2011
Copyright © 2011 A & C Black Publishers
Limited

Original concept: Paul Mason
Project management: Paul Mason
Design: Mayer Media

ISBN   HB 9781408142387
         PB 9781408142394

All rights reserved. No part of this publication
may be reproduced, stored in a retrieval
system or transmitted in any form, electronic,
mechanical, photocopying, recording or
otherwise, without prior permission of A & C
Black Publishers Limited.

The right of Jonathan Bentman and Gary
Freeman to be identified as the authors
of this work has been asserted by them in
accordance with the Copyright, Designs and
Patents Act 1988.

A CIP record for this book is available from the
British Library.

This book is produced using paper made from
wood grown in managed, sustainable forests.
It is natural, renewable, and recyclable. The
logging and manufacturing processes conform
to the environmental regulations of the
country of origin.

WARNING!
**Before beginning any training or exercise
programme, first consult your physician.
Self-defence training is potentially
dangerous and should be undertaken with
a trained instructor. Readers should not
attempt to undertake the techniques
described in this book without the
supervision of such an instructor.**

The authors and publishers of this book
assume no legal or financial responsibilty,
either direct or implied, that may result from
the use, abuse, or misuse of the information
contained herein.

Grateful thanks to:
The Jon Jepson Black Belt Academy in Derby
(www.jjbba-derby.co.uk) for all their help and
for posing for the photographs in this book,
and specifically to: Master Paul Mansfield,
Nicky Fletcher, Jason Day, Jack Wade, Harry
Filon, Georgia Cook, Nicol Winfield, Rachel
Hughes, Joti Kaur, Jake Hodgson, Aleisha
Hodgson, Richard Meynell, Kevish Ramchurun.

Photo acknowledgements
Interior photos: all by Gary Freeman, excluding
7 (right), 13 (right), 16 (top centre), all
Shutterstock

Cover photos: Shutterstock

Where appropriate, every effort has been
made to contact copyright holders of material
reproduced in this book. Any omissions will
be rectified in subsequent editions if the
publisher is given notice.

Contents

Why become a
self-defence
expert?

Ever walked down a lonely path and wondered what you'd do if confronted by a threatening adult? Or endured weeks of taunts from a school bully, wondering if there's a way out, a way to make it stop? Or wondered what would be the right moves to break free from an assailant's grasp? Then this book is for you!

LEARN TO ASSESS YOUR NEIGHBOURHOOD

Not only will you learn how to plan your route to school, to your clubs or to the shops with all the awareness of an urban ninja. You'll also learn to tune into your sixth sense, or instinct for trouble. This is because if something *feels* 'wrong', it probably *is* wrong.

AVOID BEING A VICTIM

Attackers and bullies select their victims in a particular way. This book will teach you the tricks of making yourself appear a difficult target, someone an attacker would prefer to avoid. It will give you the confidence in yourself that tells attackers: 'leave that one alone'.

LEARN TO DEFEND YOURSELF

You'll also discover some of the simplest, most effective ways to defend yourself against an attack, if the worst does happen. There are moves that can release you from an attacker's grasp, and techniques that will slow or stop your attacker, allowing you to make a safe (and speedy!) getaway.

FYI!

These features are scattered throughout the book. They contain information you can casually drop into conversation to amaze, astound, and impress your friends.

Recognizing dangerous situations will help keep you - and your friends - safer.

FINDING THE RIGHT INFO

At the back of this book there's a section called **What to do if...**, to help you identify, practice and make instinctive your reactions to a whole range of threatening situations. **What to do if...** gives you a quick-fire top 10 of self-defence actions, so that you can keep yourself, and your friends, safe. Of course, if you know exactly what you are looking for, you can just use the contents page or index to go straight to the right page.

WATCH AN EXPERT!
Throughout the book these panels point you towards web pages where you can see the relevant skills being put into practice.

Wherever you live, you can probably make yourself safer using the tips in this book.

! REMEMBER
These panels tell you one thing you should always try to remember.

LOST FOR WORDS
look here for explanations of those tricky, technical words

Self-defence techniques cannot be perfected in a day. You can only become an expert in them through long-term practice.

First principles: **avoid, escape, defend**

Effective self-defence starts long before fighting off a physical attack. Self-defence is a three-stage process. It starts with avoiding potentially unsafe situations. If it's too late to avoid the situation, making an escape is the next best solution. Only as a last resort should you have to defend yourself using physical self-defence techniques.

AVOIDANCE
A few simple tips can make it much less likely that you will ever find yourself under attack:

• Pick your route
Walk where the path or pavement is well lit and well travelled. Avoid short cuts through quiet, isolated areas.

• Walk away from trouble
If you're approaching someone or a group who are making you feel uneasy, don't force yourself to push on. Instead cross the road at the earliest and safest opportunity. Distance is a great ally in self-defence.

• Stay visible
Often we pick places to hang out because they are private, but this can put you in danger. Check out your hangout – does it also allow other people to be unseen? Do other people who use it make you nervous? Then pick another place.

martial arts techniques for fighting and defending against attack

ESCAPE

When bullied, to run away may seem cowardly. Or if an unknown person seems scary, running away may feel plain silly. But in both situations putting distance between you and a potential attacker is a brilliant idea. (Always run to safety: see page 10.)

DEFENCE

In this book we'll show you some of the most effective self-defence moves. But you will need to back this up by taking a self-defence or **martial arts** class with expert guidance. See page 40 for more information about finding a class.

SECRET TRICK

Most of us carry mobile phones, and these can be a great self-defence aid.

1 Have the phone programmed on speed-dial with your parents' numbers, so you can call them in a flash if you find yourself in a worrying or dangerous situation.

2 Always try to be aware of where you are. If you know where you are, even approximately, you're making the chances of help reaching you quickly far greater.

FYI!

Millions of people practice martial arts worldwide. The World Taekwondo Federation reports that it alone has over 70 million members.

! If you remember one thing from this section, make it:
• **Self-defence starts long before physical fighting**

Confidence and body language

An attacker will only pick on you if he or she thinks an attack will succeed, because you will not offer much resistance. Using body language, you can give off a sense that you know what you are doing, and feel confident. This will make most attackers think you are too tough a target to bother with.

> **!**
> If you learn one thing from this section, make it:
> • **Looking confident will help you stay safe from attack**

PAY ATTENTION TO YOUR SURROUNDINGS
Surprise is one of the key elements in most attackers' plans. This means not paying attention to your surroundings is a great way of becoming a victim. Never walk along with a hoodie covering your vision, looking at a narrow patch of ground, listening to an MP3, unaware of your surroundings.

WALK CONFIDENTLY
The way people walk sends off signals about how they are feeling. Walk in a way that says you are alert, confident and feeling strong:
• Keep your shoulders back, and your arms loose and relaxed
• Look ahead, not down at the ground, and stay alert and focused
• Walk with a confident, relaxed stride.
Together, these techniques are likely to put off an unknown would-be attacker.

FYI!
Attackers choose their victims using a three-stage process, known as ATP. That's A for assessment (checking you out); T for testing (challenging you with their presence or words); and P for physical (actual attack).

body language signals about how a person is feeling given off by the way they move

judo type of unarmed fighting using throws and holds

karate type of unarmed fighting using fast blows or kicks

BOOST YOUR CONFIDENCE

Bullies typically look for weaknesses in their victims and prey on these. If you lack self-confidence it may encourage a bully. Try doing something to make yourself feel more confident, for example joining a self-defence class, or a martial-arts class such as **karate** or **judo**. At these, you will develop not only your physical self-defence skills, but also your mental strength.

SECRET TRICK

At night there's one rule: never be on the streets alone. It's much safer to be in groups, or at least with one companion.

1 A lone walker on a dark night is a relatively easy victim, but a group makes a far more difficult target.

2 If you are caught out alone: avoid shortcuts and dark paths. Walk in the middle of the pavement rather than close to the edge of the road, bushes or other things that could hide an attacker.

Check out bad body language in action at:
www.acblack.com/instantexpert

Know your
safe places

! If you learn one thing from this section, make it:
- **Keep a map of your local safe places in your head at all times**

Running away from danger works *only* if you run to a place where an attacker will not continue the attack. If you know places in your neighbourhood where you can find safety, as soon as you feel under threat you will be able to think of the closest one, and run there. Here are some of the kinds of safe places it's a good idea to find and remember.

If you knew someone who lived in one of these houses, they would make a safe place to run for help or shelter.

OFFICIAL BUILDINGS
Police stations are obvious safe places, and so should be a first choice when looking for somewhere to find safety. But there will be light and other people who can help you, and perhaps even security guards, in other public buildings. Fire stations are almost always staffed and open, and so are hospitals.

FYI!
The world's cities are watched by millions of **CCTV** cameras. For example, in 2009 just one area of London, Wandsworth, had 1113 cameras trained on its streets.

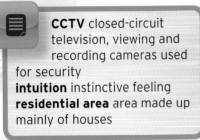

CCTV closed-circuit television, viewing and recording cameras used for security
intuition instinctive feeling
residential area area made up mainly of houses

SECRET TRICK

Plan walking routes to avoid possible danger zones. Always pay attention to your **intuition** – if a place feels dangerous, it probably is dangerous! Watch out for:

1 Anywhere that gives an attacker the chance to hide, then surprise you. Alleyways, parked cars, bushes, corners and high walls are all examples.

PUBLIC PLACES

Public places will offer the chance of help from other people, and possibly security guards and CCTV surveillance that an attacker might want to avoid. Shops, shopping centres, bus stations, cafés, pubs and bars, and restaurants are all good places to head for if you feel threatened. When you get there, call for help, or tell someone what has happened.

LOCAL KNOWLEDGE

If you find yourself under threat in a **residential area**, keep in mind that there will probably be places where you can go for help. The best places are houses lived in by friends, family members, or people you know. As a last resort, knocking on any door where there's a light on will probably be safer than staying alone on the street.

2 Isolated or poorly lit areas – any time you're not within view of other people you run the risk of not finding help should you need it. Some places are perfectly safe during some hours and very unsafe at others.

Travel **safely** on **public transport**

Each year there are many reports of physical assaults **on public transport – yet millions of journeys are made in complete safety. How can you try to make sure your journey is one of the safe ones? As always, the first rule of self-defence is to avoid danger before the trouble starts. These tips will help you travel safely on public transport.**

TRAVELLING BY BUS

During the daytime sitting anywhere on the bus is usually safe, because there will be plenty of other people on board. If you get on a bus that's mostly empty, the safest place to sit is near to the driver. At night, always sit near the driver – or at least where he or she can see and hear you.

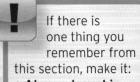

If there is one thing you remember from this section, make it:
• **Always travel in the company of other people**

TRAVELLING BY TRAIN

On trains, the carriages with the most people inside are safest. Be ready to move to another carriage if your carriage empties at a stop, leaving you alone. Do this at the stop, not once the train is moving again, and don't sit down until you are in a carriage with a good mix of people. Again, intuition will help you assess a safe place to sit. Any time you feel uneasy, just move.

TRAIN AND BUS STATIONS

At larger stations, CCTV usually monitors the platforms and **departure lounges**, making them fairly safe. At smaller stops, try to arrive just in time for your train or bus so that you are not waiting for long. Wait in the light, and try to stand with other people. If 'your' crowd leaves, be prepared to move close to another group.

If you travel alone, always try to stay near large groups of other people.

departure lounge place where people wait to catch a bus, train or plane
physical assault attack

SECRET TRICK

If you're planning a trip, why not take a friend? It's safer and more fun!

Anything that distracts your attention from the journey also reduces your powers of awareness. In addition, your phone or MP3 player might be attractive to a thief, making it more likely you will be attacked.

FYI!

A recent survey of train and bus passengers revealed that 5% of people had been threatened with violence by another passenger.

The **three Ds**

The first step in defending yourself is to avoid being attacked in the first place. Think of the things that motivate an attacker, then work out how to counter them. There's an easy way to remember and practice this, known as the three Ds of avoiding attack. They are: Desire, Decision and Distance.

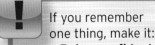

If you remember one thing, make it:
• **Being confident and alert will help keep you safe**

DESIRE
'Desire' means an attacker's desire to find a victim. Try to remember ways to avoid becoming a victim of that desire:
• Use self-confidence and body language to mark yourself out as a difficult target
• Plan walking routes so that there are no opportunities for someone to catch you alone and by surprise
• If someone seems to be gearing themselves up to violence, by shouting or abusing you, try to defuse things. Don't raise your voice, and don't return insults.

DECISION
Even if an attacker makes a decision that you are a good potential victim, he or she will only attack if success seems certain. If you stay in public places where there are other people around, and avoid isolated or dark areas, the chances are the attacker will never feel confident enough to attack you.

> **counter** act against
> **striking distance** close
> enough to hit someone;
> arm's length

SECRET TRICK

This simple trick will help you avoid being attacked by someone coming from a car.

1 Always walk in the opposite direction to the traffic. This makes it almost impossible for someone to draw alongside you, then leap out and grab you.

DISTANCE

Attackers need their victims to be within **striking distance**. If the worst happens and someone tries to assault you, try to keep as much distance between you and them as possible. If they cannot get at you, the attacker will eventually give up.

2 Apply the same thinking if an unexpected attack comes from a person or people in a car. Run in the opposite way to the direction the car is pointing. The attackers will not be able to use the car to overtake you.

FYI!

Scientists think that 60–70% of our understanding of how other people are feeling is communicated by body language.

15

Dealing with bullying

Bullying has always happened, but that doesn't make it right. In fact, in most countries bullying is illegal and can be treated as a criminal offence. Bullying still goes on, partly because it often goes unreported. How can you deal with bullying if it happens to you, or to someone you know?

WHY DO PEOPLE BULLY OTHERS?

Most bullies act the way they do because of how they're feeling, rather than because there is something about the victim they don't like. Almost always they are trying to make themselves feel less powerless by picking on someone else. Bullies have often been bullied themselves.

BEATING THE BULLIES

Here are two key ways to beat the bullies:

1) Always report bullying, whether you are the victim or just a **witness**. In the long run this will be good for the bully, too, as he or she will get help to become a better person. Tell your friends, a teacher, and your parents. It will help if you keep a record of what's happened.

2) As much as you can, try and stay clear of the bully. Play in different parts of the playground, and avoid crossing paths. Try to stay with your friends as much as possible: bullies often like to catch people alone.

suicide act of killing yourself
witness person who has seen something happen

SECRET TRICK

Cyber-bullying is a term for bullying using mobile phones, texts, emails and social networking sites. If it happens to you:

1 Take a screen grab of any Internet pages as evidence, in case the bully deletes their comments later.

2 Report the bully, as you would in real life. You'll have the proof in your phone or on your computer, so your parents, school or the hosts of the website will quickly see what is happening.

3 Always think carefully about what information you want to share with the world, especially when it comes to photos. Don't give bullies ammunition for picking on you!

BOOST YOUR SELF-CONFIDENCE
If the bully has sniffed out that you lack self-esteem or confidence in yourself, try martial arts or self-defence classes. Many people say taking this kind of class helps them to feel stronger and more confident, mentally as well as physically.

FYI!

In 2003, a government study found that 16 children each year commit **suicide** as a direct result of bullying.

Don't hesitate: run!

All of us can sense danger, it's part of our internal self-preservation **warning system.** So when you think you sense danger, it's best to take heed! Don't feel foolish – just do what's necessary to get out of the situation. One of the best ways to do this is to run away.

If you remember one thing, make it:
• **Don't let fear root you to the spot – if you're scared, run away**

The moment you feel threatened, run away before an attacker can reach you.

SAY: 'STAY AWAY FROM ME!'
Not everyone you meet is an attacker: most people are friendly. If someone comes towards you and you feel nervous, there's a simple way to find out whether they wish you harm. Just tell them to keep their distance: if you tell someone, 'Stay away from me!' and he or she keeps coming, you need to get away.

RUN – IMMEDIATELY!
The time to run is the very first moment your instinct tells you to. If you've issued a challenge and the stranger hasn't stopped, don't delay – turn and run, as fast as you can. The attacker will be expecting you to carry on talking, and will be taken by surprise.

FYI!

The fastest speed ever recorded by a running human is 26.7mph, by 100m sprinter Maurice Green during the 1997 Athletics World Championship.

SECRET TRICK

Don't let your attacker know you're about to run. Doing something that gives you a head start can make the difference between escape and capture:

1 Break away in mid-sentence, or if the attacker is close push them in the chest or throw something at them.

Giving an attacker a sudden, unexpected shove in the chest might give you time to escape.

RUNNING WEAKENS THE ATTACKER

If you don't move, the attacker will have all their energy when they reach you. If you do run, they will spend a lot of energy getting hold of you – if they decide to chase you at all. Many attackers quickly give up when their victim runs away. Also, if you're young, an adult attacker is unlikely to be as fit or as fast as you. Get going early enough, and you will have a good chance of outrunning them.

2 If you have something valuable, such as a phone or money, throw this to one side. The attacker may decide to go for that, instead of you.

self-preservation
ability to stay away from harm

Don't be afraid to shout!

Sometimes, despite all your care and planning, an attacker may catch you completely off guard. If the attacker manages to get hold of you, what can you do? Starting on page 26 we'll describe ways of fighting off an attacker and escaping. But there are other defences open to you as well – for example, shouting!

REACT QUICKLY
In the situation shown in the photos, the attacker has not only surprised his victim but also managed to grab her – but it seems there may be help nearby. Once she is in a solid hold, she is unlikely to be able to **de-escalate** the situation by talking to her attacker. She needs to **react** quickly.

USE YOUR VOICE – LOUD!
With other people within earshot, making a lot of noise may be enough to send the would-be attacker running, attract help, or both. The attacker probably won't be ready for you shouting and screaming at the top of your lungs. Yell like your life depends on it. Aim to be deafening: it may momentarily stun the attacker and weaken his or her determination, giving you a moment to pull free and escape.

If you learn one thing from this section, make it:
- **Don't be shy: shout, yell and scream to attract help**

de-escalate try to decrease the level of tension or anger
react respond to someone else's actions or behaviour
strobe brilliant, pulsing light

ASK PEOPLE FOR HELP

At first, many people are reluctant to get involved in confrontations. They will walk by rather than risk getting hurt themselves. But if you catch someone's eye and scream, 'Please, help me! I'm being attacked!' they will either help, band together with others to help, or call the police. (If you witness an attack on someone, first call the police, then tell the attacker the police are on their way.)

FYI!

The loudest recorded human shout measured 121.7dBA. It was made by Annalisa Flanagan, a teacher from Northern Ireland, in 2010.

SECRET TRICK

Personal alarms are inexpensive, and can be a very useful way of defending yourself. They may scare off an attacker, attract help, or both.

1 Alarms need to be ready to be used in a split second. A personal alarm at the bottom of a schoolbag is obviously not much use. Resting in the palm of your hand, or in your pocket, is much better.

2 Personal alarms can emit sirens or even synthesized human screams at up to 145 decibels, which is incredibly loud. Some even shine **strobe** light.

 East Dunbartonshire Council

Ignore your ego

!

If you remember one tip from this section:
• **Focus on getting away, not standing up to people**

Never miss the opportunity to escape because of your ego or possessiveness. At close quarters with someone being aggressive, your main aim should always be to get away from the situation. The examples in this section show two common situations, bullying and mugging, where ignoring your ego will keep you safe.

FIGHT OR FLIGHT?
This is a bullying situation. The bully even has a gang, so the victim is outnumbered, and in a no-win situation.

The bully is taunting the victim, questioning his bravery. 'Come on, fight - or are you too chicken?' The victim would never be able to fight three attackers.

LET IT GO
Here the victim has been distracted by texts on his phone, and was unaware of being stalked by a mugger.

Once the mugger has attacked, the safest way to act is to give him what he wants. Do not think about the cost or sentimental value of the things being stolen.

close quarters close together or near to another person or people
ego opinion of yourself and how other people should treat you

Even if there was only one attacker, it would still be safest to do what the victim does: run for it. This is common sense. To get beaten up when you could have run away is foolish.

If you feel threatened, and a mugger wants something you have, let them have it. Whatever you lose, it will not be worth being beaten up or worse to save.

SECRET TRICK

Passing something to a mugger can be an opportunity to escape, if you throw it at him or her.

1 Don't throw the item like a missile, straight at the attacker. Use an arcing lob, as if you are saying 'here - catch'. That way the attacker will have to keep his or her eyes on the kit (and take his or her eyes *off* you) to catch it.

2 You could throw the item on the ground, as shown above, so that the attacker has to bend down to pick it up.

3 The time it takes for an attacker to gather up the kit will give you time in which to escape, by running away with a useful lead.

FYI!

In the UK, there are more mobile phones than people. So if an attacker wants your phone – is it really so precious?

The **A to H** of escape

There are lots of things to keep in mind when trying to defend yourself against possible attack. Fortunately, many of the most useful tips for escaping from an attacker can be remembered using this A to H of escape:

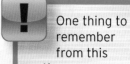

One thing to remember from this section:
• **Self-defence isn't necessarily difficult - it can be as easy as ABC**

A IS FOR AWARENESS
Be aware of who is nearby and what is happening around you.

B IS FOR BREATHE
It's normal to become tense in stressful situations. To react to a dangerous situation in the best possible way, though, you must be relaxed and ready to act. Reminding yourself to breathe deeply will help put your body into this state.

C IS FOR COMMUNICATE
Talking to someone who is acting aggressively can be a good way to calm him or her down, or at least to buy yourself some time. Or, you may need to communicate with people who might help you by yelling at the top of your lungs.

D IS FOR DON'T IGNORE YOUR INSTINCTS
Too often people ignore their instincts and tell themselves 'don't be so stupid'. But your senses could be right: crossing the road to avoid a gang won't seem so silly if you don't, then find yourself under attack.

E IS FOR ENVIRONMENT
Be aware of isolated or dark places where attackers could hide, and avoid them.

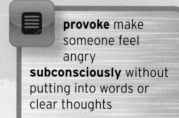

provoke make someone feel angry
subconsciously without putting into words or clear thoughts

SECRET TRICK

Never tell an attacker, 'I know self-defence' or, 'I'm a black belt in karate.' This will probably **provoke** them and, of course, it rarely sounds convincing.

Instead, let an attacker **subconsciously** read the clues in your confidence, and the way you take a defensive stance. These should put worry and doubt in their mind about whether their attack will be successful.

G IS FOR GET AWAY
If attackers can't reach you, they can't attack you. So keep your distance from suspicious-looking people. And if you have to, run!

F IS FOR SHOUT 'FIRE!'
In fact shouting anything will help. But it's said that if you shout, 'Fire!' people will run toward you, and if you shout, 'Mugger!' they'll run away.

H IS FOR HIT
When all else fails, sometimes you have to hit out in order to stun an attacker and give yourself a chance to run away. You will see techniques for doing this in the rest of the book.

FYI!
Our instincts are inherited from a time when humans could be attacked by animals or other people at any time. That's why it's never a good idea to ignore them!

Defending yourself physically

There may come a point where, despite all your precautions, you've been cornered. It becomes clear that an attack is about to happen. This is the worst possible situation – but with some well-practised techniques, you can still shock your attacker and escape.

If you learn one thing from this section, make it:
• **Always give 100% commitment to beating an attacker**

ONLY EVER USE THESE TECHNIQUES TO DEFEND YOURSELF!

MATCH AN ATTACKER'S AGGRESSION
Attackers rarely expect their victims to be immediately aggressive. If you match an attacker's **verbal** aggression by adopting an arms-up **defensive stance** (see page 30), you will be sending out a signal that you are not as easy a target as he or she thought.

TAKE CLASSES
To become a fully rounded expert in self-defence, you need to take classes as well as reading this book. The safest, best way to learn self-defence techniques correctly is through proper teaching. A good teacher will make sure that you start with the correct technique in the first place, and then pick up no bad habits while training.

defensive stance way of standing that helps defend against attack
verbal using spoken words

SECRET TRICK

The technique of hitting an attacker first then running to safety is known as 'bash and dash'. But it only works if the 'bash' happens at lightning speed:

1 Kicks to the groin can be intercepted by an attacker, and once holding your leg he or she will be able to get you on the floor very quickly.

BE FIERCE!

Once you have been attacked, defend yourself as fiercely as possible. All the techniques shown on the next 12 pages have to be executed with such power, speed and accuracy that they shock the attacker. If they are, he or she will feel like they have run into a brick wall, rather than an easy victim.

FYI!

Once someone aggressive starts talking in words of one syllable, it's a sign that his or her mental energy is becoming focused on a physical attack.

2 Ear slaps are painful to the attacker if done fast and hard, but unless they are accurate will leave your own head and body open to attack.

The **upward block**

The key to this technique is:
• **Block the attack fast, before the attacker is close enough to grab you**

stability ability to stay on your feet
deflect push aside

The moves shown here, and on the next ten pages, all come from martial arts. They are all defensive moves, which assume the first strike comes from the attacker. We show perfect demonstrations, but few attackers behave in exactly the same way as an opponent in the gym. It's important to be able to adapt techniques to different situations – only practice will give you this ability.

1) DEFENSIVE STANCE
The defender (on the right) stands with one foot back, feet about shoulder-width apart. Her body is slightly angled to the attacker, not square on. This way it will **deflect** a blow, rather than take it full force. Her stance gives her **stability** and balance. Another option is for the defender to put her hands up with open palms, as you will see in some of the techniques shown on the following pages.

2) DEFLECTION
The attacker lunges forward but the defender brings her arms up close together in front of her, then sweeps them outward, bent at the elbows. This deflects the attack, and stops the attacker getting a grip on her. The deflection hurts your forearms - but not so much as a blow to the head hurts.

3) STRIKE

The defender pushes the attacker's arms down, which means he is now moving downwards, instead of towards her. She can launch a knee at his head or chest. With strikes like this, hit *through* the attacker, not just at the surface. This will cause maximum pain and damage.

4) ESCAPE

The strike from the knee has hurt or winded the attacker, who has been stopped in his tracks. Because this is a martial arts demonstration, the defender has once again adopted a defensive stance. In a real self-defence situation, this would be the moment where you would turn and run for safety or help.

SECRET TRICK

Your arms are one of the most useful blocking tools you have, and can be used to avoid attacks to your head and upper body. But meeting an attack head-on can be painful and cause injury. These tips will help you use your arms effectively:

1 Always try to meet an attack with your arms at an angle of about 45º. This will deflect the attack, causing the force of the blow to slip along your arm.

2 When absorbing an attack, move your arm in a twisting movement, with your hand moving away from your body. This again helps to deflect the attack, and takes some of the force out of the blow.

FYI!

Expert technique can only be learned through lots of practice. To get to a black belt status in karate, for instance, usually takes a minimum of four years.

The **downward block**

Whether you block attempts to hit or grab you in an upward or downward movement depends on what feels most natural to you. If the upward sweep shown on pages 28 and 29 feels awkward, the reverse technique of blocking with a downward action, shown here, may be the best one for you to learn.

The key to this technique is:
• **Make the chin strike as quickly as possible once the block is done**

FYI!

Height and size don't mean much in self-defence and martial arts. Kickboxing champion Jean-Claude Van Damme is 5'9", and Bruce Lee, also a martial arts expert and film star, was 5'7".

1) ARMS-UP DEFENSIVE STANCE
In this situation the defender (on the right) has decided to keep her arms up and palms out as part of her defensive stance. Note that she keeps her elbows bent: this is so that if they are struck, her arms will move backwards and **absorb** the force of the blow. Her hands are open, ready to push aside an attack. One hand is a little further forwards than the other, matching the feet.

2) DEFLECT DOWNWARDS
As the attacker lunges forward, the defender swings her arms firmly downwards and out. As with the upward block, this deflects his arms outwards and drops his weight downwards. In a photograph it's impossible to show the speed and energy that is put into this action. To succeed, it must be a split-second action made with a lot of force and determination.

3) CHIN STRIKE

The defender delivers a strike to the attacker's chin with the **heel** of her palm. She uses the hand that was drawn slightly back: by twisting her hips and shoulders forwards, she adds to the force of the blow. With the whole weight of her body behind the strike, it will be extremely painful for the attacker. In a real-life situation, this would be the moment to run away and look for safety or help.

absorb take in or soak up
condition get used to, or become able to perform an activity more easily than you could before
heel pad at the base of the foot or hand

SECRET TRICK

Learning to block blows effectively takes a lot of practice. Blocking techniques are not pain-free, and at first your arms will be sore after practising. You may even pull out of blocks at first because you are nervous about the pain. This soreness doesn't last forever!

1 The only way to overcome the pain is to practice: this will **condition** your arms to the sensation of pain.

2 Once you have conditioned your forearms, your blocks will become powerful – so powerful that they are almost a form of attack, since they will allow you to throw an attacker off balance.

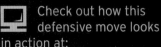
Check out how this defensive move looks in action at:
www.acblack.com/instantexpert

The **combined** up-down **block**

The key to this technique is:
• **Perform this block with great speed, to confuse your attacker**

Here is another variation on the block, which is especially useful when an attacker comes at you with both arms. You can use this block to lift one of an attacker's arms while pushing the other downwards. This leaves the attacker open to strikes that will slow down or immobilize him from various directions.

FYI!

Because the jawbone is close to the inner ear (which affects our balance and orientation) a hard strike to the jaw will cause an attacker to lose balance.

1) OPEN HANDS OR FISTS
The defender (on the right) has made her hands into fists instead of putting her palms towards the attacker (as on page 30). She also has the backs of her forearms angled towards the attacker. There is no right or wrong way to put your hands in defensive stance, but open hands are more defensive. A closed-fist stance tells an attacker you are ready to fight.

2) BASH AWAY THE ATTACKER'S ARMS
As the attacker lunges forward, the defender bashes his arms away with maximum possible force. Combining the techniques from pages 28 to 30, she forces one up and one down. As long as she has her defensive stance correct, with her feet shoulder-width apart, this destabilizes the attacker but has almost no effect on her own balance.

SECRET TRICK

When striking an attacker, it's usually best to hit him or her with the heel of your hand.

1 Hitting with a clenched fist may cause you to injure yourself with a sprain, or even broken bones, leaving you weakened.

3) STRIKE – AND STRIKE AGAIN

The attacker's head is open to a strike, so the defender swiftly chops her left hand into his neck. While his head is travelling downwards, she meets it with a palm strike to his jaw. In all her techniques the defender's feet stay **planted**: she gets power into her strikes by twisting at the hips. These two blows should be enough to weaken an attacker, and allow her to make a speedy escape.

2 Hit your attacker's chin with the heel of your palm, gaining force by rotating your hips and shoulders before striking under the jawbone.

immobilize prevent from moving
planted rooted to the ground; immovable

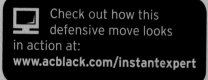

Check out how this defensive move looks in action at:
www.acblack.com/instantexpert

The **sideways block**

This block is useful when defending yourself from a powerful punch that an attacker has aimed at your head. You use both arms to deflect the blow, so even strong attacks can be defeated. In this instance the attacker has led his assault with a right arm punch aimed at the head. His attack is blocked, and his 'victim' quickly hits him twice.

1) WATCH FOR THE PUNCH

The first photo shows an attacker (on the right) drawing back his right arm, ready to punch or make a grab at the girl's head. This gives her a warning that the attack is coming, and she has a split second to get ready. As the punch comes in, the defender turns her hips and shoulders to the left, towards the punch. She lifts her arms, ready to deflect or block the punch.

2) STRIKE BACK

Because the defender has extended his arm in a punch, his head and neck are open to a **counter strike**. Starting from the blocking position, the girl whips her arm back at the attacker, hitting him with an open-hand palm strike to the chin.

> If you remember one thing about this technique, make it:
> - **Twisting your hips adds force to both strikes**

3) LAUNCH A SECOND STRIKE

The first strike against the attacker has caused the girl's hips and shoulders to swing round to her right. She can use the **momentum** of this movement to strike at the attacker a second time. She does this by bringing round her left arm, following up the right with a second palm strike to the attacker's jaw.

adrenaline rush
sudden release by body of natural drug that causes the heart to beat faster
counter strike strike in response to an attack
momentum combination of movement and power

SECRET TRICK

In an attack situation it's normal to experience an **adrenaline rush**. This can cause you to freeze up and be unable to act. But it will help to know that an adrenaline rush is actually a good thing.

Music with a lot of beats per minute can cause the body to release adrenaline. That's why it is often played in gyms. Getting used to doing things while feeling the effects of adrenaline will help you to control yourself in a self-defence situation.

FYI!

Adrenaline makes your heart beat faster. The sudden release of adrenaline is a natural reaction, intended to allow you to deal with dangerous and unexpected situations.

Check out how this defensive move looks in action at:
www.acblack.com/instantexpert

Slip, slap, slop

This is a very quick move that has to be practiced hard. It is a good way to deal with a punch, especially a punch thrown wildly at your head. It uses the orientation of the attacker's body to force him or her off balance. This makes the attacker vulnerable to a counter strike that may give you time to escape.

1) SLIP THE PUNCH

The girl on the right has already decided she plans to defend herself by slapping away an attack, so while in defensive stance she has her hands facing her **assailant**. When the attacker tries to use his right hand to punch her in the head, she blocks the strike with her forearm. Keeping her elbow high allows the blow to slide along her arm. This block will not completely stop the punch, but will slow the blow down enough for the rest of the technique to work.

2) SLAP THE ATTACKER'S ARM DOWN

The girl then slips her arm round to the other side of the attacker's arm. This has to be done extremely quickly to work, so it has to be practiced again and again. Gripping his right arm with both of hers, she guides the attacker's movement downwards. This uses the movement the attacker started by throwing the punch to expose his **torso**.

The key part of this technique is:
- **Slip your arm around the attacker's forearm super-fast**

WARNING!

Never practise self-defence techniques on your friends: someone will get hurt. Go to a class, where there are mats and other safety gear.

3) SLOP - STRIKE WITH THE KNEE

As the attacker's torso rocks downward, the girl brings up her right knee to strike his body. This knee strike has to be done very quickly and with as much force as possible. It will then injure or wind an attacker, who will struggle to chase after you.

assailant person who launches an attack
torso part of body between neck and legs, not including arms

SECRET TRICK

All self-defence techniques work best at speed. The speed at which you make physical movements is controlled by your brain and nervous system. It can be trained to react more quickly:

1 Practise techniques slowly at first - almost in slow motion. This gives your mind and body a chance to learn the technique 100% correctly.

2 Once you have learned the technique, steadily increase the speed at which you do it. Eventually you will build up a physical memory that allows you to perform the technique very quickly, almost without thinking.

 Check out how this defensive move looks in action at:
www.acblack.com/instantexpert

Attacks from behind

Statistics say that most attacks come from in front, but attackers do sometimes come at their victims from behind. Often, attackers wrap their arms around victims in a 'bear hug', trying to pick them up and drag them off. The technique shown in this section allows you to deal with a bear hug.

1) NO TIME TO REACT
You rarely see an attack from behind coming. Even if you have a sense that there's someone behind you, it's almost impossible to do anything before being grabbed. In these photos, the attacker has grabbed his victim around the middle and locked his hands before she has time to react.

2) BREAK OUT OF THE BEAR HUG
The defender raises her hands and hooks them inside the attacker's forearms, pushing down and away. She also drops her weight towards the floor and forces her hands down hard enough to break the attacker's grip. To make this technique work you have to throw yourself downwards with great determination. Just leaning your weight against the attacker's arms won't work.

butt hit someone using the head

3) LAUNCH AN ELBOW STRIKE

With his grip broken, the attacker is no longer pressed against the defender's back. She has room to twist around and deliver an elbow strike into his face. Alternatively there are other counter attacks available in this situation: scraping the attacker's shin hard, stamping on his or her feet, or **butting** your head backwards into the attacker's face, for example.

FYI!

Bears do not use bear hugs to crush their prey to death. They usually stand on their back legs, and swipe with their paws and claws.

SECRET TRICK

Sometimes an attacker coming from behind will pin your arms at your sides. Even then, there is a technique for escaping.

1 Very quickly, roll your shoulders up and inward. The aim is to lift your elbows upwards too.

2 This will give you a little bit of space, just enough to bring your elbows sharply backwards into the attacker's stomach. An alternative to this technique is a sharp backwards jab of your head, into the attacker's nose.

 Check out how this defensive move looks in action at:
www.acblack.com/instantexpert

Learn and have **fun** with **martial arts**

Self-defence blends naturally with martial arts. The techniques in martial arts often work well in self-defence situations. Martial arts also improve alertness and confidence, which gives an extra layer of self-defence. If you are alert and confident, you are less likely to need to use your self-defence techniques in the first place.

BENEFITS OF MARTIAL ARTS

Learning a martial art is demanding, and to be a good student requires a lot of hard work. This hard work has measurable rewards, though. Your self-defence skills improve, of course. Students often also find that their grades in school or college improve when they start working hard at martial arts. Working hard and seeing successful results also helps people to feel more confident.

Another benefit of learning a martial art is that it will teach you the **dynamics** of body movement. This not only helps with self-defence, but also makes you much more effective in other sports. For example, you might learn the angles at which your leg kicks most powerfully, which could come in useful when playing football.

FIND THE RIGHT MARTIAL ART FOR YOU

There are lots of different martial arts to choose from. Many clubs allow a free trial before you join, so you can try a few different **disciplines** before making a choice. Here's our guide to some of the most popular martial arts:

Karate: probably the most popular martial art, karate teaches mostly defensive techniques, including blocking, punches, kicks and throws.

Judo: in judo the emphasis is on defence. A *judoka* learns to use an opponent's strength against him or her, turning an attacker's energy into a throw.

Jujitsu: similar to judo, jujitsu is said to have developed from the need to defeat an armoured enemy by throwing him or her to the ground.

Kung fu: kung fu features chops, kicks and throws, but the discipline also focuses on the mental aspect of fighting.

Taekwondo: the emphasis in taekwondo is on kicking techniques, but powerful punches and other strikes are also taught.

MMA: this stands for Mixed Martial Arts, and is growing in popularity very quickly. MMA mixes up all kinds of martial arts in one exciting package.

FYI!

In martial arts, teachers and other students must always be treated with respect and good manners. Anyone behaving badly risks being asked to leave.

discipline form or type of martial art
dynamics way that movement produces force
judoka student of judo

What to do if...

Some self-defence situations crop up more often than others. You're much more likely to be faced with a dark walk home than someone leaping out of the bushes in front of you, for example. This list outlines ten of the most common scenarios, and gives some ideas for how you could deal with them.

1 You've been delayed leaving school, it's dark, and your usual route home is through a park.
First call your parents to let them know you've been delayed and where you are. They might offer to pick you up. If not, then plot a new route that cuts out the park and offers a safer - even if longer – route. Tell your parents the route you'll use, and if you can, walk with a friend.

2 You are walking your usual route, but there's somebody ahead who your senses suggest looks menacing.
Trust your senses, and alter your path to avoid the threat. Cross the road, or turn around and take a completely different route. Look to see how many people are nearby, to make sure you're not alone. When changing your route make it look deliberate, maintain a sense of confidence, and stay a good distance from the menacing person - even if you have to run to do it.

3 You're on a train, it comes into a station and many people get off. You're left with one man opposite you. Your senses may not be suggesting you go to full alert, but you feel a little nervous.
Don't wait, get up and change carriage straight away. If the man is innocent it won't matter to him. If he isn't then you're moving to safety. It's important to be alert and assess the situation as it happens. Don't wait until the train is moving out of the station to move. Do it while the train's still at the station, so that it looks like you might be getting off.

4 Your school bully has you cornered and says he or she wants your phone/MP3 player/lunch money.
Let them have the phone. But pass it to them in the most distracting manner possible (see page 23) and try to run away. Then immediately report the theft to a teacher.

5 You're walking along and sense you're being followed.
If the distance isn't already too close, turn around and tell whoever's behind to stop following you. If they're innocent they will stop coming toward you. If they take another step, assume they're a risk and run. If they're already very close behind you, just run. You can check if they're still following once you've reached a place of safety.

6 You're walking home when a car pulls alongside you. The person or people inside start to hassle you.
React immediately. Turn around and run in the opposite direction from the car. Don't talk back, just get away.

7 Someone in a car calls you by name and says your parents asked him or her to pick you up. The person knows your parents' names, where you live, and even knows your dog's name.
Do not get in the car. This person could have found the information anywhere. Stay a safe distance away from the car. Never be embarrassed by refusing to get in. No one with good intentions will force you to get into a car if it is clear you do not want to. If they do try to force you in, run away while calling for help in a loud voice.

8 You're leaving the cinema or some other event late at night with your friends.
It's tempting to let your guard down when you're feeling happy, as if nothing could go wrong while you're having such a good time. But still, take a look around you. Most people should be going home or arranging their next activity. If there's someone nearby who's just hanging around, he or she could be an attacker.

9 You're walking down a street you don't know, and you start feeling uneasy.
Maintain a sense of confidence and purpose, and don't try to hide in the shadows. Walk in the middle of the pavement, stay away from parked cars, and leave a good gap between yourself and high walls or blind corners. Do not panic, but scan for safe places that you might run toward if something happens.

10 You're starting to feel paranoid. You've read this book, and suddenly the world feels very intimidating and dangerous.
Don't worry! Attacks are very rare, and almost everyone gets through life without ever being assaulted or attacked. At the same time, a little bit of knowledge, planning and common sense can go a long way towards keeping you safe. And a martial arts or self-defence class might make all the difference if you do find yourself in a dangerous situation.

43

Technical self-defence language

absorb take in or soak up

adrenaline rush sudden release by body of natural drug that causes the heart to beat faster

assailant person who launches an attack

body language signals about how a person is feeling given off by the way they move

butt hit someone using the head

CCTV closed-circuit television, viewing and recording cameras used for security

close quarters close together or near to another person or people

condition get used to, or become able to perform an activity more easily than before

counter act against

counter strike strike in response to an attack

de-escalate try to decrease the level of tension or anger

defensive stance way of standing that helps defend against attack

deflect push aside

departure lounge place where people wait to catch a bus, train or plane

discipline form or type of martial art

dynamics way that movement produces force

ego opinion of yourself and how other people should treat you

heel pad at the base of the foot or hand

immobilize prevent from moving

intuition instinctive feeling

judo type of unarmed fighting using throws and holds

judoka student of judo

karate type of unarmed fighting using fast blows or kicks

martial arts techniques for fighting and defending against attack

momentum combination of movement and power

physical assault attack

planted rooted to the ground; immovable

provoke make someone feel angry

react respond to someone else's actions or behaviour

residential area area made up mainly of houses

self-preservation ability to stay away from harm

stability ability to stay on your feet

striking distance close enough to hit someone; arm's length

strobe brilliant, pulsing light

subconsciously without putting into words or clear thoughts

suicide act of killing yourself

surveillance camera a viewing and recording camera used for security purposes

torso part of body between neck and legs, not including arms

verbal using spoken words

witness person who has seen something happen

Further information

BOOKS

Know the Game: Judo Geof Gleeson
(A & C Black, 2004)
Know the Game: Jui Jitsu World Jiu Jitsu
Federation (A & C Black, 2004)
Both books explain the core skills,
tactics and rules of the discipline, with
plenty of information, photographs and
illustrations.

The Shotokan Karate Bible
Ashley P Martin (A & C Black, 2007)
An authoritative 208-page book that
guides students through everything they
need to know about karate, right up to
gaining black belt status.

The Mixed Martial Arts Handbook
John Ritschel (A & C Black, 2009)
Explains how to perform a variety of
martial-arts techniques, most of which
are useful in self-defence.

WEBSITES FOR ADVICE ON BULLYING:

www.bullying.co.uk
www.childline.org.uk
Both these websites aim to protect
children from harm, and have advice on
what to do and where to get help if you
are being bullied.

CONTACTING MARTIAL-ARTS ORGANIZATIONS

These sites will enable you to find a club
or class near where you live, either by
emailing them or using a find-a-club
search engine:

www.nakmas.org.uk - the National
Association of Karate and Martial Arts
Schools

www.thebka.co.uk - website of the
British Karate Association

www.feko.co.uk - the Federation of
English Karate Organizations

www.bccma.com - the British Council for
Chinese Martial Arts (Kung Fu)

www.britishjudo.org.uk - the British
Judo Association

www.bjjagb.com - the British Jujitsu
Association

www.btcb.org.uk - the British Taekwondo
Control Board

www.britishtaekwondocouncil.org - the
British Taekwondo Council

Self-defence timeline

776 BC to AD 400
Olympic Games in Greece include martial arts such as wrestling, boxing and pankration (a combat sport that included aspects of wrestling, grappling, throws and boxing).

500-400 BC
Bodhidharma (an Indian Buddhist monk), often said to be the originator of Eastern martial arts styles, arrives in Shaolin-si (China). He teaches Zen Buddhism, including body and mind exercises that will form the basis of martial arts.

300-200 BC
Styles of Chinese martial arts such as Hsing-i begin to develop distinctive forms.

AD 500
The Shaolin Monastery, in China, said to be the place of origin of kung fu, is founded.

1100
The Japanese warrior class, known as samurai, emerges during a period of war between the Taira and Minamoto families. The samurai will last 700 years.

1447
On the Japanese island of Okinawa, King Sho Shin bans the carrying of weapons. Local warriors immediately begin to develop unarmed fighting techniques that are still used today in karate and jujitsu.

1700
The distinctive Wing Chun kung fu style begins to develop in China.

1877
The law governing self-defence in the USA is created, in a case called Runyan v. State.

1882
Professor Jigoro Kano develops a variation on traditional Japanese jujitsu, which he calls judo. It becomes the first Asian martial art to gain worldwide recognition, and will later become the first Asian martial art to be an Olympic sport. Kano would one day be Japan's representative on the International Olympic Committee.

1893
Edward William Barton-Wright studies jujitsu in Japan. When he returns to England, Barton-Wright begins to teach what he calls bartitsu, a blend of Asian and European fighting styles.

1900
British and American soldiers begin to learn martial-arts techniques for unarmed combat from the Japanese Army.

Immigrants from the Japanese island of Okinawa begin to settle in Hawaii, USA, and start teaching karate to local people.

1905
Mitsuyo Maeda, a student of Jigoro Kano, travels to the USA and gives demonstrations of judo to American universities, the US military and wrestling clubs.

1907
Maeda travels to the UK and again demonstrates judo. He shows judo's effectiveness by fighting with wrestlers much larger than himself and winning.

1972
The Buddhist Shaolin philosophy and Kung Fu is popularized in western culture through an American TV series called *Kung Fu*, which tells a story of a Shaolin monk, Caine, as he travels through the American West.

Judo becomes an official Olympic sport.

1973
Chinese-American actor and martial-arts expert Bruce Lee popularizes karate and martial arts in the western world through the film *Enter the Dragon*. Age 32, Lee died the same year after suffering a swelling of the brain.

1914
Maeda settles in Brazil, where he pioneers judo techniques. Today he is known as the father of Brazilian jujitsu.

1935
'Karate' is adopted as the official name of the style of martial arts developed on the Japanese island of Okinawa.

1945
World War II ends. Many returning British and American soldiers bring home martial arts learned in Asia, and demand for martial-arts classes increases.

1949
China brings all its martial arts forms together under the name 'wushu'.

1957
Korea brings all its martial arts forms together under the name 'taekwondo'.

1967
The (British) Criminal Law Act 1967 is passed. It makes changes to the law relating to self-defence, and says that: 'a person may use such force as is reasonable in the circumstances in the prevention of a crime'.

1984
The film *The Karate Kid* grosses over $90 million in box-office receipts, becoming another martial-arts blockbuster. The film tells the story of a teenager who is bullied, but with the help of an Okinawan immigrant learns karate (and its lessons for life), overcomes his bullies and wins the local karate tournament.

1988
The legal case of Beckford v. R (1988) establishes the principle of self-defence in the UK: 'a defendant is entitled to use reasonable force to protect himself, others for whom he is responsible and his property. It must be reasonable.' The law also says, 'A man about to be attacked does not have to wait for his assailant to strike the first blow or fire the first shot; circumstances may justify a pre-emptive strike.'

2000
Taekwondo becomes an Olympic sport.

2008
Wushu is demonstrated during the Olympics in Beijing, although not recognized as an Olympic sport.

Index

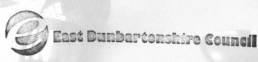

East Dunbartonshire Council